I WANT TO KNOW WHAT L♥VE IS

A
BRIEF
BOOK
ON
LOVE
LONELINESS
AND
COMPULSION

SAUL ROSENTHAL

authorHOUSE®

AuthorHouse™
1663 Liberty Drive
Bloomington, IN 47403
www.authorhouse.com
Phone: 1 (800) 839-8640

Published by AuthorHouse 03/09/2016

ISBN: 978-1-5049-6685-6 (sc)
ISBN: 978-1-5049-6683-2 (hc)
ISBN: 978-1-5049-6684-9 (e)

Library of Congress Control Number: 2015920628

Print information available on the last page.

This book is printed on acid-free paper.

To Karol Sue, the music of my heart.

I should have been a pair of ragged claws
Scuttling across the floors of silent seas.

T.S. Eliot
"The Love Song of J. Alfred Prufrock"

Yes, he was at the end ... Might the fishes devour him,
this dog of Siddhartha, this madman, this corrupted
and rotting body, this sluggish and misused soul! Might
the fishes and crocodiles devour him, might the demons
tear him to little pieces! ... Then from a remote part of
his soul, from the past of his tired life, he heard a sound.

Hermann Hesse
SIDDHARTHA

In my life there's been heartache and pain
I don't know if I can face it again
Can't stop now I've traveled so far
To change this lonely life
I want to know what love is
I want you to show me
I want to feel what love is
I know you can show me

Mick Jones
"I want to know what love is"

PREFACE

Next to Anais Nin's journal of 170 volumes (published and unpublished), my 3000-page uncut confession measures more like an anecdote. In an age driven by speed and brevity, however, 3000 pages is encyclopedic. I have opted, therefore, on a distillation of sorts that is easily consumable in a few hours. Boiling down seven decades to get at the essence of a less than heroic life is not easy.

G. B. Shaw once apologized in a letter to a friend that he did not have time to write a shorter letter.

I have taken time. I hope it is worthy of yours.

Many years ago I read a few words that cut me to the quick: "Love does not exist . . . ." Perhaps among the saddest words imaginable. They were written by, of all people, Robert Penn Warren, one of America's foremost literary figures. Significantly, he qualified it: "but the dream of it does."

It needs more qualifications -- maybe even refutations. In the first place, he can only be referring to romantic love, or the ideal of it evolved especially since medieval and Renaissance literature (although it is really as ancient as the oldest legends, myths, songs and epics of mankind) as well as the late 18th and early 19th century, the great age of the Romantics.

Dr. Warren cannot be referring to all types of love, for that would be blatantly absurd.

The many forms of love are the magic of reality, not just the stuff of dreams, that holds our hapless lives together, that keeps us clinging to the life-preserver of hope when

3

the odds and the facts are against us, and keeps us from drowning in despair and killing ourselves.

Lest us start with the love of God and the love of art. The two are often connected. They have richly fed each other. Religion has inspired much great art; perhaps most of it throughout history if we consider its Influence in Oriental and Semitic countries as well as ancient Greece, medieval and Renaissance Europe, and other Western examples. Oriental temples, the Parthenon, Chartres, Notre Dame, St. Peter's Basilica and St. Paul's Cathedral come to mind. Also the great epics and the literary and poetic aspects of the Bible, as well as other holy books. Michelangelo, DaVinci, Raphael, Handel, Bach, Milton, and countless others were inspired to surpassing works of art by their faith. In turn these works have filled countless mortals with a love of God.

There is also the love of nature and the love of country: like religion, no small solace and inspiration throughout history to both artist and non-artist.

I shall exclude such propensities as the love of pizzas, Mickey Mouse, Elvis, Doonesbury, wind surfing, hang gliding, golf, French fries, blue jeans, jellybeans, and kosher pickles, although the passion may be as great, or greater, than nobler loves. Clearly there are many varieties, degrees and dimensions of love.

Let us stay with the larger or less watered-down implications, which bring us to the love of humans. Maternal love first comes to mind as perhaps the most powerful and lasting. Other blood relationships are often no less intense, whether sibling love, the love of a grandparent, grandchild, niece, nephew, uncle, or aunt. Non-blood relationships, however, are often where the troubles begin. For years I have squirmed under the weight of Warren's cynicism (not overall cynicism, of course, but as related to the problem) and have, as a result, come to be more critical of it.

Evidence abounds on my side: Robert and Elizabeth Barrett Browning, Will and Ariel Durant, Heloise and

Abelard, Edgar Allan Poe and Virginia Clemm, Anthony and Cleopatra, George and Martha Washington, Franklin Roosevelt and Lucy Mercer, and, dare I mention, whatever their peccadilloes, Ronald and Nancy Reagan.

I might also add the romantic liaison of G. B. Shaw and Ellen Terry. "Let those who may complain that it was all on paper," wrote the famous playwright, "remember that only on paper has humanity yet achieved glory, beauty, truth, knowledge, virtue, and abiding love."

Because romantic love does not last in 99% of couples (am I *really* that cynical!), we cannot say it does not exist at all. For the most part it seems more a matter of rhythm, of ebb and flow, of waxing and waning, of flourishing and fading, much as the cycles of nature: sunshine and night, warmth and cold, summer and winter, birth and death. Or perhaps less regular at times: quixotic (after Don Quixote), quicksilverish, spontaneous, eruptive, impulsive, or demented. In short, dynamic -- like a growing

thing, organic, and therefore ever mysterious, illusive, and elusive, and ever more desirable, precious and beautiful.

But let me come down to earth again. Literally the good earth. I often walk (and sometimes jog when my old bones and back don't complain) through cemeteries because the earth there is fair to see and fine to feel underfoot, always tended with great care and the landscaping often done with great artistry. In the many years I have sauntered through these cemeteries seeking composure, solitude, resuscitation, exercise, fresh air, the sun, the ambience of nature, the endless islands of beautiful flowers (mostly plastic) brought by the mourners, I have thought about the visitors, many of whom come frequently and not just yearly. At first I said to myself how utterly, utterly idiotic of these poor fools to waste precious time, the most precious gift on earth, just to tidy up the gravesite or dress it up with flowers, plants, or shrubbery. Over the years the fidelity of these visitors of all ages, many of whom are husbands or wives or other non-blood relatives of the deceased, has

come to make me far less contemptuous of what I once saw as silly obeisance to a few old bones, which we are all destined to become. A far, far better thing, I thought, would be to reverence, to celebrate, like Albert Schweitzer, the eternally rich and diverse profusion of life all around us. There, surely, is holiness and indwelling divinity.

But the persistence of the devoted and unfailing visitors convinced me at last that I had missed the heart of the matter, which was not a blind ritual of honoring old bones with flowers that either quickly wilted or, in the case of the plastic ones, were gathered up by the attendants and discarded or were scattered, broken, or soiled by wind, rain, snow, and ice. The heart of the matter, at least as I felt it, was that Warren's denial of love was wrong and that I myself was the fool for not seeing it sooner, or understanding sooner that it was not to be seen in flowers or gravestones chiseled with lachrymose poems or bromidic sentiments, but in the enduring love that brought the mourners back again and again. Hardly a delusion

or a figment of their imagination, but a tug as real as the moon's tidal pull on the oceans of the world.

In the cemetery, the undying reality of love was an awakennng moment. Paradoxically, it was also a moment of profound depression. My past flashed before me like a film gone awry and racing madly. I saw that I had been shut out my whole life from the total kind of love experienced by the faithful mourners.

I refer to those related not by blood but by marriage. The love of close relatives and friends most people have experienced. Blood relationships and platonic friendships sustain us in times of great crises, stress, failure, bereavement, or other tragedies. But rarely do they offer the solace of a lover to a beloved, united as they are in the flesh as well as the spirit.

One out of two marriages fails, and of those that last, few of the couples continue to share their affections in the countless little ways of intimacy that young lovers

spontaneously display. ·Yet these happy few remain a constantly envied ideal of most of us, or at least those of us whose lust for life has not turned to ashes.

It is the very frustration of this passion for completion that makes so much of our lives miserable and drives us into compulsions that enslave or destroy ourselves as well as others. The fortunate loners find happiness in creative works, religion, sports, avocations, making money and other sublimations to compensate for the lack of love or the loss of it. Still, secret desires die hard and I imagine it is our fantasy life that more and more becomes our release valve, as the years mount, and saves us from the implosion of a breakdown, suicide, or other disasters of the mind or body.

No wonder that in the darkest years of the Depression, Hollywood thrived.

THE GLASS MENAGERIE, Tennessee Williams' first full-length play (and one of his best), takes place during that dark decade of the thirties. Since it is loosely based on the writer's family, the character of Tom betrays attributes similar to those of Williams. He is sensitive to a fault and a gifted, intelligent, highly imaginative young man who writes poetry and obsessively escapes to the fantasy world of the movies to avoid an irrepressibly dominant (but good-hearted) mother, a shy, pathologically introverted and crippled sister, and a humdrum job in a warehouse.

Admit it or not, the dream factory of Hollywood has been the salvation of many of us. Growing up in the 30s a child of a struggling family, I can remember the one overweening joy of my life was the weekly Friday night Western or Saturday matinee.

Like Williams' Tom, I became an accomplished, if not compulsive, escapist. I remember, some years later, seeing a French film that was thought too wicked and

banned in New York before the courts allowed it. The title was *LA RONDE*, or round dance, after a play by Arthur Schnitzler called *REIGEN*. It was directed by Max Ophuls and starred the elite of the then-popular Gallic actors. So utterly enchanting was this brilliant, bittersweet, and naughty comedy about the whimsicalities and infidelities of love that I could not leave the theater. I arrived for the first showing of the film at 11 a.m. and left after the last, around midnight. The year was 1950.

It took hours to readjust to the real world. Frankly, I don't think I ever did, or wanted to, so disenchanting was the contrast. "The art of life is the life of art," said Henry Miller.

The real world was not exactly what I had in mind in my pursuit of happiness. At least it was not right for me. Or I for it. The philosophy of Auntie Mame -- "The world's a feast and all you poor SOBs are starving to death" -- sounds great, but I could never seem to find out where in hell the cornucopia was located.

Hemingway made more sense: "Life breaks us all and then makes us strong in the broken places." The battle scars become our medals of honor.

For over 30 years I have read a score of books on positive thinking, starting with Napoleon Hill's *THINK AND GROW RICH*, Dale Carnegie's *HOW TO WIN FRIENDS AND INFLUENCE PEOPLE,* and Norman Vincent Peale's *THE POWER OF POSITIVE THINKING.* In recent years there must be a thousand of such books strumming on the same theme. I've read many of them and listened to the shrinks, health and fitness experts, and other hucksters of instant and easy happiness hyping their books.

As much as I've tried throughout the years, the guilt and agony resulting from my stupidity or sins have not disappeared.

Fulton Sheen, Norman Vincent Peale, Billy Graham, Robert Schuller, Oral Roberts, Pat Robertson, and a host of other persuasive or flamboyant celebrities have brought

help and happiness to millions upon millions. The New Testament idea of being reborn in an instant, or being granted instant forgiveness for all sins and a guarantee of eternal salvation merely for belief in the Messiah, are offers not easily ignored.

But neither are the less euphoric visions of Sophocles' *OEDIPUS*, Shakespeare's *KING LEAR*, Ibsen's *GHOSTS*, Sartre's *NO EXIT*, Camus's "Myth of Sisyphus," Becket's *WAITING FOR GODOT*, Hersey's *THE WALL* and SchwarzBart's *THE LAST OF THE JUST*.

The thinking man is forever condemned to a battlefield where hope and despair contend. Easy answers, immediate absolution and unalloyed happiness either in the here and now or the hereafter are suspect. If we could in fact divest ourselves of all our sins of commission and omission, venial and mortal, and all the pain and misery that stubbornly persist, merely by a trick of the spirit or verbal assertion; if our inglorious past is not only forgiven

but forgotten (see Isaiah); if all things shall pass away and all become new once we are creatures in Christ, what becomes of our individuality, our duality, the tensions and tragic dimensions that make for evolutionary struggle and spiritual growth? If our past as well as our memories are obliterated, do we not become lobotomized? "Without the hurt, the heart is hollow," according to a popular ballad.

Is it blasphemous to suggest that growth is essential to happiness, whether in this life or another, and must be a dynamic struggle?

Battle scars cannot be disavowed. Sin, suffering and failure are the only way to wisdom, to the perfection Hermann Hesse writes about in *SIDDHARTHA*.

> The world, Govinda, is not imperfect or slowly
> evolving along a long path to perfection. No, it
> is perfect at every moment; every sin already
> carries grace within it . . . the Buddha exists in

27

the robber and dice player, the robber exists in the Brahmin. During deep meditation it is possible to dispel time, to see simultaneously all the past, present and future, and then everything is good, everything is perfect, everything is Brahmin. Therefore, it seems to me that everything that exists is good – death as well as life, sin as well as holiness, wisdom as well as folly. Everything is necessary, everything needs only my agreement, my assent, my loving understanding; then all is well with me and nothing can harm me. I learned through my body and soul that it was necessary for me to sin, that I needed lust, that I had to strive for property and experience nausea and the depths of despair in order to learn not to resist them, in order to learn to love the world . . . to leave it as it is, to love it and be glad to belong to it.

Inspiring words, but for me a bridge too far to love the world as it is and leave it as it is. Despite many efforts over the years, it has not been easy to embrace the positive aspects of either Oriental or Western religions, though the struggle goes on. I guess I have always had a deep-seated prejudice that a larger love must be rooted in a personal love . . . something I sorely missed.

Yet I was not without early exposure to those whose love of God precluded mortal mates. At the Catholic University of America in my hometown of Washington, I studied the humanities. What impressed me then beyond the sophistications of philosophy and theology was that those priests and nuns, or novitiates, who led the most austere, studious, and prayerful lives, seemed the happiest. Over the past half century, this impression has not been diminished but strengthened after studying ascetics of many faiths. Philosopher and transcendental poet, Henry David Thoreau, stated well the paradox: "A man is rich in proportion to the number of things which he can afford to leave along."

Those who shunned the ratrace, took vows of poverty, and lived simply abstemious lives in convents and monasteries or dedicated themselves to the sick and needy, did not seem to be failures, nor plagued by all the mental and physical problems others were, and achieved a serenity, a positive attitude, and a happiness rarely achieved by those caught up in the competitive and acquisitive scrimmaging of life.

In spite of exposure to the exemplary aspects of religion, philosophy, and literature, I seemed not to be on the side of the angels. Being the child of an atheist mother and a communist father, I was oriented otherwise. My earliest search, not unlike most youths, was for "profane" love. Unfortunately, matriculation in the school of hard knocks did not help the search. My father, whose life was as marred by failure and depression as mine was destined to become, hooked himself up to a gas pipe in the basement of our D.C. home one day when I was 11 and my brother 13, tried to suck away his life and all its torments, and ended up a catatonic schizophrenic in a series of unsavory

mental wards. The trauma of the experience, plus what seemed hopeless years of dead-end visits to mental asylums (primitive by today's standards), were a blight upon his sons not easily forgotten.

Mental problems and maladjustments seemed to dog our family. Was I a victim of genes or events? Or both? Whatever the cause, failure darkened my days and frustrated the search for love.

The early trauma, plus economic hardship for the family, left me frightened, neurotic, and reclusive. Anxiety problems hindered concentration and school studies. I was placed in a high school remedial class for those with retarded reading ability. Stomach disturbances became severe, kept me out of the Army, and remained sporadic. Despite a desperate need, I had only a few dates during my teenage years.

How well I remember my first ill-fated crush. It happened in the 10th grade. (Nowadays there are kids in the 4th, 5th or 6th grade who play a dating game, or an approximation of it.) I sat behind a girl I thought to be the loveliest creature on earth. Giant dark eyes, sedate but warm, soulful and with a soupcon of mischief, long shiny black hair flowing over her shoulders in large waves, and a skin so spotlessly white it highlighted her full lips and smiles.

I wrote poems about her, saw her in my waking and sleeping dreams, forever ached to be close to her, or for any kind of casual friendship, so I could exult, even for a moment, in the sensuous music of her eyes and the enslaving spell of her smile. (Love does not exist, Mr. Warren?)

Alas, oh, wicked, wicked fate that spoiled a closeness I craved. I guess I came on too strong. Peons are not made for princesses. She was ever aloof but kind those long and callow years of love's lusts, and my hurt never went away. Years later when I read in Browning's "My Last Duchess"

how possessive the Duke was when his wife's smiles went everywhere (but not to him), I thought of my duchess and felt a twinge of empathy for the envious husband. At least until he extinguished his wife's generous smiles, along with her life.

My first crush left me crushed. The lessons -- or lesions -- of love come hard. In the years that followed, I learned that I was never to be counted among the inamoratos.

In "At Seventeen," a hauntingly beautiful song, Janis Ian knew well the desert in the heart of teenage rejects.

> The world was younger than today
> and dreams were all they gave for free
> to ugly duckling girls like me
> We play the game, and when we dare
> to cheat ourselves at solitaire
> Inventing lovers on the phone
> Repenting other lives unknown
> that call and say 'Come dance with me'

and murmur vague obscenities

at ugly girls like me, at seventeen

Like a moth at a flame, I did not quit easily, but the pain of reality soon seared away the innocent dream.

I plunged into an early marriage that was foredoomed to failure. My wife and I were pathetically ignorant and inhibited. Clerking at retail shops, going to college full time, and trying to adjust to a marriage in a small, two-room, roach-ridden apartment with a mother-in-law included, left me an emotional and physical wreck. After a divorce, losing my job, and ricocheting from one job to the next, I decided to try writing. At the University of Iowa's program touted for creative writers, I flunked playwriting. (The drama later won an award in a national competition. So much for academic gurus.) My only solace was that Tennessee Williams, who wrote *THE GLASS MENAGERIE* while a student there, was told he would never make it as a playwright.

I did not fare so well as a writer, though I have tried with many plays over the years. It is hard to live with constant failure when you have your heart set on something and no other talents or ambitions. I took high school teaching jobs and a temporary job at American University. While there, I continued to attach myself to failure, the worst of my life. I developed a pathological compulsion that has lasted for 25 years: gambling.

I took a teaching job at Northern Illinois University so I could gamble at the seven racetracks in and around Chicago. I gambled day in and day out on the weekends, holidays, and vacations when I wasn't busted, and I was busted more often than not. When I was in the chips I bet big. Bigger than many of the millionaires I knew in the last 25 years, which is nothing to boast of. Millionaires are notoriously tight-fisted as railbirds.

As a teacher I was not affluent, but, like many compulsive gamblers, I denied myself the smallest luxuries so I could

play the ponies. All I ever had for transportation were old junkers worth less than a thousand bucks. I lived in the cheapest single rooms I could rent. I ate out of cans. All so I could bet big. I often blew my paycheck in one day. Once you get in the habit of going to the 50 or 100 buck windows, it's hard to switch to the 2 or 5 buck windows. But switch I did when I was down. A compulsive needs action, even if it's tossing pennies, matching dimes or playing poker for pocket change.

When I was loaded I traveled. Spent thousands on air fare and gambled in just about every racing state east of the Mississippi and a few west of it. Yet all the while lived as austerely as any monk.

The urge to gamble was far stronger than the desire for such frivolities as good food, housing, clothing or cars.

One day at Arlington Park near Chicago I made $5,500, mainly on Prince Majestic, which I liked because he was

sired by Majestic Prince, a nag I won a bundle on in the Derby in 1969. Instead of being ecstatic, I was steaming with rage because, were it not for a stupid blunder in the 9th race, I would have ended up $9,000 ahead for the day instead of $5,500. Win or lose, the greed is insatiable.

I gave it all back before the week was out and couldn't afford a can of beans. Got picked up for swiping a few small packages of peanut butter crackers in a supermarket and banned for life from it.

I started gambling to escape my addiction to past failures and then became addicted to the failures of gambling. Like an alcoholic desperately trying to kill a hangover with more booze or a junkie hyping himself out of the shakes with more poison, I gambled to escape the disasters of gambling. A ghastly image somehow got stuck in my mind (I think it is from Sartre's *THE FLIES*) that seemed to fit -- that of a wounded and broken warhorse twisting and fouling its own entrails the harder it tries to right itself.

My late nemesis -- did I choose him or he choose me? -- was a very bright, crafty, cool-headed English prof and author with a penchant for the ponies and a passion for playing with numbers. Did I forget "avaricious"?. We met at American University when I became a neophyte instructor. I was flattered to be made privy to an "unbeatable" system he devised over years of study (including trips to the Library of Congress to comb through reams of past results and statistics in the daily racing pages), a strategy so flawless, so mathematically impeccable we could not fail to become frequent winners and filthy rich. It would be no sweat. Like plucking low-hanging fruit.. Money in the bank.

I swallowed it all as if it were apple pie instead of a slow, torturous poisoning that would last for years. According to my sagacious mentor, the records he examined over the previous 20 years proved with unerring accuracy that certain kinds of horses would win at certain times under precisely calculated conditions, allowing us to make big and consistent killings. As it happened, we were the ones to get

49

suckered. 20/20 visions of the past are no cinch for the future. The hard reality of uncertainty breaks the best of dreams. I concocted dozens of super-systems. On paper. None worked for this compulsive gambler any better than "moderate" drinking for the drunkard, limited smoking for the tobacco fiends, or pill popping for the overweight. All are hooked on excess. As Oscar Wilde quipped, "Everything can be indulged in to excess. Including moderation."

The gambling addict gets his kicks from action -- a built-in formula for failure, win, lose, or draw. Trying to gamble smart is seductive. But gambling junkies, like other junkies, need their hormonal rush. Not patience, not a phlegmatic cool-down, not the steel nerves of restraint. In spite of addiction to losing, gamblers continue to cook up clever systems that only lead to clever ways to lose. Brilliant mathematics that morph into fool's gold. To my astonishment, I discovered years after my father died of leukemia, he worked out a gambling system, not unlike my mentor at American University, after painstaking

research. What chilled me to the marrow of my bones was the thought that I was somehow predestined -- or at least predisposed like alcoholics or junkies -- to become compulsive since my grandfather was also a gambler, a notoriously reckless one who deserted a young wife and five children in favor of the life of a wastrel. Megalomaniacs can't be bothered with such trivial distractions as a wife and kids. My uncle, the oldest child, started to support the family at the age of 12 by delivering newspapers.

In recent years an increasing body of knowledge suggests we are far more programmed by our genes than was suspected. Couple hereditary with powerful environmental influences and one wonders just how much free will we have. Sartre, an atheist, and orthodox believers both insist we are radically free to choose. However ennobling or inspiring, it is hard to square such extremism with the brutal realities of life.

OMNI magazine some years ago interviewed a biopsychologist by the name of Jerre Levy. She is "one of the few theoreticians in neuroscience today."

> *OMNI*: You seem to be saying that all freedom of choice is biologically based and genetically wired into the brain. Isn't it paradoxical that we are doomed to make choices?

> Levy: I do say this, but I don't think there's a paradox. But it certainly does give people a lot of philosophical difficulty. The reason is that we're all obsessed with freedom, especially in America. We imagine that freedom implies that at any given moment, absolutely nothing restricts or determines what we will do -- not our genes, our biology, nor our history. We are free to override all influences on our lives and act independently of them. If we had that kind of so-called freedom, we'd be free of all the

millions of years' worth of information about the world that's been stored and incorporated and realized in our brains and minds. Totally free of all our experiences of the world, we'd be completely random systems, out of contact with any possible information that could govern directed action. Pure randomness is pure entropy, and the human brain represents a piece of material organization in space and time that has the highest *negative* entropy that we know of in the universe. So people aren't at all free in the sense most of them imagine. They're imprisoned by their brains.

The more I ponder my own erratic bungling ways, the more I am convinced I was not just weak in will power but brain power as well. I dare say many of us feel the same way. Our freedom and our fate are strongly determined by the limitations of our physical equipment.

Bluntly put, I was not right in the head and needed a shrink. But at the time I was too crazy to see that I was crazy. I was too busy trying to run away from myself to look back, too busy escaping from past miseries to realize I was rushing into worse miseries. Most of all too stupid or neurotic or cowardly to face the bitter truth that at the heart of my loneliness was lovelessness.

I blindly opted for panaceas, only to discover that sex for money was worse than no sex at all. It is to the spirit what disease is to the flesh. Yet after a hard day's gambling in Chicago on both the thoroughbred track in the afternoon and a standardbred harness track in the evening, there was no place to go to heal the fiscal and psychic wounds inflicted by the ponies other than the sleazy dives of Cicero (where Al Capone and his pals once reigned), the ugly, dingy, smoke-filled honky-tonks and strip joints promising sweet young flesh for the asking. Beyond the neon nudes on the outside, on the inside, not quite.

Instead, you might find the droning of slow, out-of-sync jazz from an old black combo, bored, bleary-eyed, and robotically grinding out tired old strip standards like "Alley Cat" and "That's Life" until break time when raucous but danceable jukebox rock filled the gap for menopausal ecdysiasts listlessly doing their thing, clinging to their jobs though gone to fat, their aging faces masked with garish paint, their eyes, sunken, sad, and bloodshot, they sashayed back and forth across the stage, undulating over-fed bellies, carelessly off the musical beat, and as they disrobed, exhibiting all the erotic pizzazz of one about to hit the sack for some shuteye. Better by far for the hungry eye that the fallen flesh stay hidden.

If only one were "noseblind" to the odors that assaulted the nostrils . . . sweat-soaked bodies and clothes, whiskey-besotted drunks with breaths as fierce as fire-breathing dragons, stale carcinogenic grease from the griddle burned over and over again under overdone burgers . . . smelly tobacco smoke burning the eyes and polluting the

lungs . . . bartenders seemingly impervious to it all, as they "wash" glasses in a soapy sink and rinse them in another with semi-clear water, all the while pestering the barflies to buy more drinks or else telling them to "get lost" when their money ran out. Pugnacious bouncers bum-rush the pathetic imbibers onto the street as reward for emptying their pockets to an old barkeep pissed off at having to listen to the same old racetrack B.S. from whining losers seeking no more than a sympathetic ear for solace. But they get back only a sneer or cynical wisecrack from the scrooge behind the bar, bent on pushing more sauce for more cash. Even as the B-girls do to the barflies between stints on the stage, oosing passion and a tongue in the ear of their targets, reeking of cheap cologne, batting eyes heavy with mascara, sparkles, or makeup to hide the sags and wrinkles, pressing their bodies close, nuzzling low-cut, pushed-up boobs into their victims, lasciviously pawing them, pleading for a drink, for a string of drinks, pretending to down the shots while spitting them back to stay sober and keep bilking the boozers . . . while teasing into their

ears that love's for sale in the back room for a 20-buck quickie trip to paradise. Or more cash if she can finagle it. Maybe even roll them too if they're smashed out of their skull enough. If any complaints follow, there's always customer service. AKA the bouncer.

If ever there was a vestibule to Dante's moral decay, a gateway to perdition and despair, it was these sordid dives sucking in the forlorn, the lonely, the loveless, smitten with every addiction, aching for companionship, an anodyne for years of psychic pain, needing but a listening ear, the touch of a kind hand, or the ersatz love behind it. For a price, of course.

I too was among the luckless seekers, forever chasing after the four-legged fillies as a consolation prize that brought no consolation, only more pain, frustration, and failure. What a morbid, senseless, masochistic squandering of precious years, but for a hopeless compulsive hooked on horses, there was no exit to a decent social life, only

the soulless and delusional gang of obsessive racetrack handicappers, driven by greed, believing the way to winners and wealth was by plumbing and deciphering the secrets hidden among the copious stats in our Bible, the Daily Racing Form.

All an insanity of unreality that became our reality. And from that specious and failed reality, I could only escape each night to a reality no better.

Still, I yearned to know and befriend those sad old strippers and hustlers who had seen better days, and also the occasional neophytes, hot young chicks with slender, supple, erotic bods. More likely than not, pimped by boyfriends to exhibit their gifts for fast and easy cash. Untutored and not without the shine of innocence, they were too callow to tease with wild abandon the salacious skills of the old pro's of the business. But soon they learn to excite the famished ids and learn as well that fresh and nubile flesh commands a generous premium.

So they split to chase a big-time showbiz dream in New York, Vegas, or L.A. Leaving behind their pals or pimps in pursuit of "exotic" stardom . . . thankful to escape the joyless pandering to horny old hooch hounds drowning their titillated lust in too much booze.

I was left with my obsession to probe the pathetic lives of the old-guard strippers and hustlers. Like a pathologist exploring the inner demesnes of corpses, I delved into their empty, blundering, debauched and drug-driven lives, their early years and ambitions gone awry, their hated parents, broken homes, broken marriages, their abortions, their alimony and multiple child problems, their pimps and hooker-years, and their abuse and exploitation in and out of jail.

For years I was determined to be a novelistic chronicler of their feckless, aimless, misspent lives (the way William Kennedy, the Pulifzer Prize winner, wrote about the dregs and rejects of Albany). Year after year I had the dream,

made copious notes, but, as Lorraine Hansberry wrote, "A dream deferred dries up like a raisin in the sun."

Despite all their wanton self-abuse, their rudderless lives, they were immersed in the raw stuff of life. Shut out from love, fatherhood, a family, close friends and consumed by gambling as I was, I fed with an envious appetite upon their impetuous passion for life. If only I could be a part of the tangled soap opera of their lives, no matter how tawdry, their lusts, their loves, their quarrels and breakups, their heartbreaks and resilience. I fantasized myself into their daily melodramas, boarded the crazy carousal of their circular and up-and-down lives, their heady commitment to nothing but the pain-killing moment fueled by the aphrodisiacs of addiction, whether alcohol, pot, drugs, smoking, or fat-rich junk food, but please, God, spare them what I have suffered for so many empty years: the addiction that yields no fiendish gratification for the flesh, unless it be the masochism of self-torture that is gambling.

Like those I mischievously envied, let me be inside the gallimaufry of life, no more the sterile pedagogue outside looking in, but rather a miscreant of emotion, obedient to the hot demands of the flesh, to the villainy of lust, to the madness of love . . . whether gone right or wrong.

Better even a broken love than ever an empty heart.

I was sick of being agoraphobic all my life, a termite hiding in the woodwork of failure and self-contempt, unloving and unloved, while others fearlessly plunged into the exaltations and agonies of life, heeding well all the demands of body and spirit to live to the fullest, to go with the imperative, intuitive call of the heart to burn brightly. To feast on time instead of killing it. To celebrate life for no reason other than the gift of it . . . before the heavy doom of time betrays it all as a vanishing dream, a sad charade.

Teaching was only a day job for me. Hardly the stuff of life. Edward R. Murrow said his father once told him

never to trust anyone who makes his living with his mouth. Pedagogues, preachers, and politicians fit the profile. But so do prostitutes.

Was I born to be a worm, a mole, forever afraid of the light of freedom, or did I willfully commit myself to it because of my weaknesses and failures? Did I choose an evasive, reclusive, fretful and absurdly compulsive life or did it choose me? I am not like Billy Joel's "an innocent man," but at the same time I cannot blame myself for failing as a playwright. Nor can I blame myself for never wanting to be anything else and therefore trying to kill the unkillable pain of failure by chasing after the bangtails.

But I have belatedly come to accept that not all losing efforts, while lesser than the winners, should be seen as failures. Muhammad Ali may well have been the greatest. But does that mean that all other contenders are failures and deserve no praise or merit for giving their all and utmost in the game of life? Should not the best within us

be sufficient for the pride, the self-acceptance, the self-respect, the self-love that we seek?

Still, the weight of failure had lain heavy upon me.

The horse, alas, may have chosen me for a ride to relief.

That salvation turned out to be but a new damnation.

A man's work comes before love. With women the latter before everything. Condemned by the ineradicable stigma of failure, I was ashamed to love; I did not know then its saving grace, its gift of healing that Bernard Malamud captured so well in "The Magic Barrel," one of his best stories, about two failures made whole by love. One was a rabbinical student, a lonely, lost and guilty misfit, not unlike myself, and the other was a rebellious, passionate, and promiscuous girl bitterly rejected by a strictly orthodox Jewish father.

Many of my best years, best love, best hopes and ambitions I gave to the horse. The single obsession of my life was to win enough to buy a horse, then more and more, and become a trainer. In the late fifties I became a groom or stable boy at Brandywine Raceway in Delaware and worked for a prominent owner of a stable of harness horses. I learned to be a driver and discovered that sitting in the sulkies behind a half-ton of muscular flesh was empowerment like no other.

Those few short summers were the happiest days of my life. But my dreams never came to fruition. I tried so hard to realize them by making money via gambling that I supplanted the dreams with an addiction and self-destructive love. Namely, the complex fascination and seduction of handicapping. An unwinnable moth-versus-flame madness that never ceased to fire up my hormones and pound my heart like racing hooves pounding the turf.

I wonder now if my love of horses was the result or cause of my retreat from human love. I suspect the truth is mixed. In any case, I soon realized my obsession enslaved me. I was deifying the noble coursers, making of them an object of veneration, of worship, of love for their beauty, their strength, their burst of power and speed, and the gracefulness of their several gaits. All obediently in the service of their masters. (But far less so in the service of the bettors, I bitterly discovered. How dare my beloved beasts betray me so cavalierly!).

I read voraciously about them, studied their history, the many breeds, their diseases, their many uses throughout history. No other animal has served man so well, so faithfully, and was so indispensable to our progress throughout the history of civilization. It's as if the Creator perfectly designed a horse to suit the needs of man as a beast of burden and for travel, just as in the Genesis fable He creates woman to suit man's needs for a loving mate.

And yet, I confess, a thousand times when they busted me, or lost by a nose or a neck, I cursed them with a hatred every bit the equal of my love. Such is the toxic spawn of addiction. It corrupts the wonders of the world and turns those joys into contempt. Contempt as well for the addict himself.

In the seventies, after several years of gambling, I realized I was possessed of a terrible disease that was metastasizing like a cancer into every aspect of my life and was eating out all the joy and vitality. I started with Gamblers Anonymous and continued with it for two decades. It was not a quick cure. It only helped me to quit sporadically. Especially when I was flat-ass busted and down psychologically.

I sought help from a county clinic, a psychotherapist, assertive training groups, and holistic health workshops. Bad habits die hard. . They erode the spirit like a virus. But die they must if we would live.

We know now that constant stress and anxiety can cause serious, even fatal, diseases. In the early 1980s, my prodigal ways culminated in a fiscal disaster and mental ordeal that I thought would break my gambling monomania.

For years I have been loaded with loans, a constant source of pressure and worry since I was forever hard put to pay them back and pay them back dearly, since interest rates of loan companies are unbelievable. I have paid as high as 40% per year. But the bite never made any difference when I needed money, which was always.

Living under the gun half of one's life is bound to take its toll mentally and physically. And so it has. No less so the damage of living a lie year after year, ever fearful of students, teachers, and administrators discovering my hypocrisy and sick double life.

The humanities deal with values, among other things, and because of my secret betrayal of many of the essential ones and the resulting baggage of guilt I have condemned myself to, I have gone out of my way to stress their importance my entire teaching career, which coincides with my gambling history.

A number of times I have run into students of mine at the Chicago, St. Louis or Louisville tracks. Such moments have been the most excruciating I can remember, since honesty, a value that I stressed with my students, compels me to admit that gambling is basically immoral because it corrupts you into thinking that to get something for nothing is okay. Is this the right value to inculcate in children -- that everything in life is luck and hangs on a roll of the dice? TV game shows and quiz shows incessantly drum that into our heads. If you're lucky enough to be born with genes that make you attractive or handsome, lucky enough to have the gift of gab and a personality on steroids, lucky enough to get chosen for those shows, and lucky

enough to beat the others at silly games or give the right answers, you deserve to win thousands, hundreds of thousands, even millions. This daily obscenity of dumping tons of unearned money on the lucky ones is being broadcast by all the major and minor media to hundreds of millions, if not billions, nearly every day. While half the world would be happy with a piece of fruit, a bowl of soup or a clean glass of water. Life is a crapshoot. Why bust a gut working hard? Gamble! Like the TV says, you too can be a lucky winner of $5000 every week for the rest of your life.

Totally demented dreamers, who line up for blocks, wait hours, and swear they have as good a chance as anyone else, seem to forget that the odds of winning a billion bucks are 1 in 292.2 million.

Gambling is the number one pastime in America, as well as other countries. Eighty percent of the people in America gamble. Estimates vary on the number of compulsives,

but the likelihood is close to 10%. In view of the damage I have seen done to compulsives over the past 25 years, in terms of broken homes, broken health, lost jobs, penury, and the pressure to take up other compulsions, alcoholism, smoking, excessive eating, drugs, prostitution, forgery, stealing, embezzlement, etc., I cannot wax ecstatic over the explosion of lotteries and other forms of gambling that are being legalized throughout the country. And the world.

But enough of fine sentiments and sermonizing. I had better stick to my own story. Non-compulsives are turned off by recovered compulsives preaching against the evils of addiction after they have beaten theirs.

As my debts over the years grew larger and larger, my delinquencies grew worse. In the 70s I grew more desperate, traveled to other cities for loans, falsified applications, wrote bad checks, hocked everything that wasn't nailed down, took to lying to the bank and loan officers with a straight face (though my conscience was

burning, since I had never done such), and borrowed from friends (a particularly painful maneuver since I was single and should have been far better off than they financially).

As a result of my high-flying shenanigans and losses of over $400,000 over the years, too many loans and $50,000 in debts (not a great amount to many but far more than I could handle on my salary at the time), I crash-landed. I borrowed from banks, loan companies, the credit union, credit cards, and friends. When you're desperate for cash to feed your addiction, you lie. As a result of the stress, I developed chest pains, chronic gastritis, ulcers, headaches, and depression, I could no longer function, no longer get out of the sack some mornings to go to work.

My attorney recommended bankruptcy. In spite of 25 hellish years of incessant financial crises, I never once entertained the idea of bankruptcy. It seemed utterly insane. I had a steady job, I had no family to support, nobody was holding a gun to my head demanding I blow

my paychecks year after year at Chicago, Cincinnati, Detroit, Louisville, Keeneland, and St. Louis racetracks.

All I had to do was stop gambling and pay off my debts. It was as simple as that. At least on the surface. Deep down I knew I was victim to a terrible disease (now recognized as such by associations of psychologists, psychiatrists, and physicians), every bit as serious as alcoholism or drug addiction.

My creditors did not see it that way, which is why I went through two years of harassment before bankruptcy was family granted by the court. To my dismay I discovered that not only many creditors regard compulsive gamblers as degenerates, but many others, including some friends, look upon them, unlike other addicts, with equal contempt.

As depressing as this revelation was, I can understand why prejudice survives in spite of the hard clinical evidence. I was a victim of the selfsame delusion when I started gambling. It took me several years of heavy gambling

before I could face the fact that I was compulsive. Even after I started going to Gamblers Anonymous, I resisted for months the simple admission that all members made at the very beginning of their weekly confessions. Namely, that they were compulsive gamblers and had no control over their lives as such. (Gamblers Anonymous, like many other support groups, is indebted to the pioneering therapy of Alcoholics Anonymous.)

At the very first meeting of Gamblers Anonymous I remember I was appalled when members confessed they had been compulsive gamblers for 25, 30, even 40 years. I figured these guys were nuts. Such idiocy could never happen to me. I thanked my lucky stars I got to the meeting in time to put the fear of God – or an unholy Hell -- into me. After 25 years of gambling, I was still enrolled in the school of hard knocks. Like my compulsive colleagues, I was a slow learner. My only dubious distinction: promoting myself to the bizarre kicks of a full-fledged masochist. I have punished myself in guilt and self-contempt for so

long because of my failures and weaknesses, I had grown addicted to self-flagellation.

In the subsequent years, however, in a desperate effort at self-analysis and self-therapy, I had become a determined learner about compulsions. Mine and those of others. I have read widely on the subject and kept a journal that is now close to 3000 pages. There have been some maniacal relapses that I cannot comprehend, but much less than before. I am not now cured nor will ever be. All the experts indicate compulsives are never cured and must be on guard every single day of their lives. Not a happy prognosis. Nevertheless, I cherish the dream of every tortured compulsive: to be forever free of the plague that rots body, mind, and spirit, and to build an immunity to new infections of an old disease that has led many to suicidal depression..

Early trauma, neuroticism, and anxiety led to failures and learning problems, which led to more emotional turmoil,

which led to more failures. I early on became a bona fide misfit and ended up, early in life, a confirmed escapist living the hit-it-rich dream of the gambling addict that always turned into a nightmare. However belated my efforts, I figured the time had come to use my God-given brain -- or Darwin's version of it -- for something better than wantonly wasting it. After all, it took about four and a half billion years of Earth's history to evolve a brain. That merits some respect, if not awe.

I became a compulsive student of compulsion. I attended most of the support groups that allowed my presence and pondered the many and complex causes of addiction to overeating, alcohol, tobacco, drugs, prostitution, white-collar and other crimes (rape, wife abuse, child abuse, thievery and arson). As a result of volunteering to teach extension courses in Illinois and Indiana prisons, I learned more about compulsions.

Each compulsion obviously has its unique and peculiar cluster of causes (perhaps, at least partially, rooted in heredity). There are, however, many strikingly similar, if not fundamental, causes that apply to many groups. For this reason, I proposed to a number of leaders occasionally joint meetings of compulsive groups.

After visiting many groups, I concluded that the sharing of ideas and the crossfire (support groups are often shocking, soul-wrenching, even brutal) would be of some value to compulsives of every variety.

Another reason I favor a collective gathering is that attendance in each group fluctuates a good deal, which leads to a small membership that becomes very inbred. I discovered, sad to say, that some who attend regularly for long months or years ironically end up reinforcing their maladies. Like bulimics who binge-purge so they can pig-out repeatedly.

The vigorous rap sessions can serve as a weekly absolution, like a visit to the confession box or a hellfire-and-damnation sermon on Sunday, so they can start afresh their cycle of self-abuse. Compulsives can unwittingly become addicted to a therapy which fortifies their addiction – a paradoxical rationale that allows them to assuage their guilt and continue their bad habits at the same time, rather than break clean of the addiction and eliminate the need for the therapy altogether.

I believe a mixing of divergent groups of addicts and the injection of new blood could well bring greater insights via an exchange of narratives peculiar to each addiction.

Whatever new approaches are attempted -- and there seems to be an endless stream of new books on ways to combat compulsion, especially overeating -- habits ingrained over half a lifetime or during the early years don't vanish overnight. The social or behavioral sciences I believe are not science at all and should be referred to as studies

since individuals are infinitely complex, often hopelessly unpredictable, and forever proving the experts wrong, In spite of the perplexities and controversies surrounding irrational, masochistic, or criminal behavior, choices have to be made, both by adult victims of disorders and parents who must try to prevent such problems in their children.

I don't have any miraculous answers, but were I king of the world -- make that president (the world has enough tyrants) -- I would have appointed the late Dr. Leo Buscaglia as my Minister of International Education. For all his flamboyance and media-friendly style, his message deserves serious attention. From our earliest years we are not taught how to love -- the many ways, verbal and physical, of giving it as well as recognizing and receiving it. Instead we are shackled with all the inhibitions, constraints and taboos of our parents, who, in turn, were emotionally stunted by their parents.

In a chaotic, violent, and polluted world where most of the young, no less than the environment, are being corrupted as never before, thanks to the good old lust for power and profits, parents do not have an easy job today. Even for the ideal parents. And most are not so ideal, as a result of violence in the home (one in five families), divorce, single parent homes, working parents, teenage parents, alcohol, tobacco, pot, or cocaine-addicted parents, addiction to over-the-counter pills, junk foods, TV and video-game violence, online porn, shallow reading habits, etc., etc. Small wonder that delinquency, crime and compulsions are rampant throughout the land.

Parents are too busy with their own ego trips or too indifferent for other reasons to take care to love their children and teach them how to love in return, how to express their love and how not to be ashamed of it.

Research and statistics substantially prove that Dr. Buscaglia was not blowing hot air. Animal studies, for

example, demonstrate that offspring deprived of affection become physically as well as emotionally stunted, more neurotic and more aggressive. Caring, loving, profoundly committed parents do not generally raise dropouts, runaways, hell-raisers, delinquents, teenage prostitutes, dopeheads, and terrorists.

But saving the world, Dr. Leo Buscaglia, that compassionate and ebullient crusader, the "doctor of love," could not do any more than the Messiah of love, despite 2000 years of His message. The world is never saved -- only individuals are. Which means I had better come off my high horse of pedanticism and concentrate on the failings and betterment of my own life.

Bankruptcy and Buscaglia got me off the high horses of gambling and onto the pursuit of human love. The transition from 4-legged fillies to 2-legged ones was not easy. While working at Brandywine Raceway during my early years of gambling, I developed a love for the steeds that exceeded

anything I ever felt for a woman. For a non-fantasy woman, that is. Since my background was in literature, there were women aplenty to love from afar, from the goddesses of ancient Greece to the goddesses of Hollywood. But after a neurotic and anxiety-ridden early life with very few dates and a bad marriage, I soured on the mating game altogether and opted for a rich fantasy life instead. This included not only the movies, erotic literature and art, but a fascination with department store and clothing store mannequins, which developed into far more than a passing fancy. I spent afternoons walking about studying these artifacts with an obsessive interest in the beauty of their faces, whether idealized or individualized.

I was driven to meditate on the nature of beauty as did the old German in Thomas Mann's *DEATH IN VENICE* -- Aschenbach was his name. He was hopelessly smitten with the beauty of a young Polish boy named Tadzio, but only platonically, esthetically, ethereally.

I began collecting photographs, drawings, and paintings of the faces of beautiful women, which I came to worship with the zeal of a pilgrim before a sacred shrine. Is not beauty in this world a living testament to the holy work of Creation? Khrushchev's proclamation that got worldwide attention during his visit to the United States -- female faces were more beautiful than their bottoms -- was hardly an epiphany.

As much as I loved the beauty of horses, especially horses in motion, and most especially those astonishingly talented white horses of the Spanish Riding Academy of Vienna, the Lippizaners, they could not compare with the pulchritude of female physiognomies. At least in the eyes of most human spectators. Amorous hippos, crocodiles, giraffes, turtles, porcupines, or platypuses have their own esthetic sensibilities.

My obsession with mannequins hardly seems a unique propensity in view of the extraordinary popularity of dolls

over the years. To the frustrated lover or romantic or child in us all, the proximity of three dimensional beauty is a special turn-on. It can stir the blood like nothing else, perhaps because few are lucky enough to possess, or even get close to the magnetism of beauty that is alive, and therefore we gladly settle for the closest approximation.

We live by our illusions and sometimes are saved by them. The dreamer is deep in us all, is even quintessential to our nature, for without the dream we would still be living in trees and caves instead of voyaging to the stars.

In younger years I wrote skits about a plug-in prof and about robots in love. Later about a youth consumed with a passion for a mannequin who comes to life. Such a fantasy is hardly unique. Since the mythology of ancient Greece, there have been many examples from the folk literature of different cultures dealing with the miraculous transformation of inanimate (and animal) forms into humans. Bold flights of imagination, the stuff of legends, epics, and

fairy tales, have been man's way of compensating for the boredom, the bludgeonings, the sorrows, and the longings for love we are condemned to.

The frustration and defeat of the impulse to love is the genesis of much of our misery (as well as violence and crime). It is the great destroyer of our precious innocence, of the child in us that is the generator of hope for growth and faith in ourselves. To re-awaken love is to empower us to build that faith into a fortress of the mind where we are the makers of our own happiness.

The old saying, "Life begins at forty," is rendered obsolete by our increasing longevity and vitality. Dr. Ashley Montagu, distinguished anthropologist and author of *GROWING YOUNG*, insists we are never too old to begin anew. I am convinced that learning to love and relate to humans is essential to his dream of growing young.

Arthur Clarke's prediction of immortality for the human species may be feasible, given the quantum leaps of medical science and technology. But as of now we are still mortals, and as radically as the future may change our physiology, our environment, and even our very nature, we cannot deny our immediate essence.

For it is this essence, our mortality, the fact that we must suffer, must grow old, and must die, that determines our values and our happiness. Central to these is love. Love and death are intimates. For it is our very mortality that makes of love the most precious potential we share on earth.

Shakespeare says it best in his sonnets. The following is 73.

> That time of year thou mayst in me behold
> Upon those boughs which shake against the cold,
> Bare ruin'd choirs where late the sweet birds sang.
> In me thou see'st the twilight of such day

As after sunset fadeth in the west,

Which by and by black night doth take away.

Death's second self, that seals up all in rest.

In me thou see'st the glowing of such fire

That on the ashes of his youth doth lie,

As the death-bed whereon it must expire,

    This thou perceiv'st, which makes thy
love more strong,

    To love that well which thou must leave
ere long.

George Chapman, a friend of Shakespeare, as well as poet and playwright, wrote the following passage on love in his play, *ALL FOOLES*. It epitomizes the ideal of impassioned romantic love like few poetic works before or since.

    I tell thee Love is Nature's second sun,

    Causing a spring of virtues where he shines;

    And as without the sun, the world's great eye,

    All colours, beauties, both of Art and Nature,

Are given in vain to men, so without love

All beauties bred in women are in vain;

All virtues born in men lie buried,

For love informs them as the sun doth colours,

And as the sun reflecting his warm beams

Against the earth, begets all fruits and flowers;

So love, fair shining in the inward man,

Brings forth in him the honorable fruits

Of valor, wit, virtue, and haughty thoughts,

Brave resolution, and divine discourse.

Oh,'tis the Paradise, the heaven of earth.

The New Testament passage on love from the "First Letter to the Corinthians" (about 55 A.D.) is not by a romantic poet but by Paul, an itinerant preacher for the new faith, yet it is no less intense in praising that sacred passion. The following is from the Modern Library translation.

I will show you a far better way. If I can speak the languages of men and even of angels,

but have not love, I am only a noisy gong or a clashing cymbal. If I am inspired to preach and know all the secret truths and possess all knowledge, and if I have such perfect faith that I can move mountains, but have no love, I am nothing. Even if I give away everything I own, and give myself up, but do it in pride, not love, it does me no good. Love is patient and kind. Love is not envious or boastful. It does not put on airs. It is not rude. It does not insist on its rights. It does not become angry. It is not resentful. It is not happy over injustice, it is only happy with truth. It will bear anything, believe anything, hope anything, endure anything. Love will never die out . . . . Faith, hope, and love endure. These are the great three, and the greatest of them is love.

Khalil Gibran wrote that in discovering truth we discover ourselves. Having won that wisdom, we need only the

courage to be happy, to reach out with love, to be a hugger in the spirit, if not the flesh. Dr. Martin Luther King, Jr., spoke of that courage to be happy, to reach out with love. Though he was humiliated, beaten, jailed, and assassinated, his words endure: "I have decided to stick with love, because hate is too heavy a burden to bear." And so is self-hate, failure, and guilt over all my transgressions, all my sins of commission and omission. Said Freud, "Guilt must be pierced like an abscess." No more than this freedom is my secret desire. I could die happy in such a victory. For only love can take the sting out of death.

In reaching out to others, we reach out to the ideal, we honor our loving nature and pay obeisance to the Source of that loving nature, to that Power behind all power, to that sweet Mystery beyond all science and reason, to the eternally awe-filling, magical, dynamic, and infinitely fecund manifestation of Spirit that infuses and energizes the mightiest of galaxies that flood the farthest reaches of the cosmos.

Blessed, immeasurably blessed indeed are we happy few, beneficiaries of an eonic and macroscopic evolution. We are distant sparks struck off from a divine forge, children of an unfathomable, ineffable Maker or Matrix that we are impelled to love as Father/Mother Creator and to perpetuate that inimitable miracle of love that gave us birth.

Noblesse oblige!

Love is our humble ritual of worship in a cosmic cathedral for the greater glory of God. A God that is either eminent or (as that God-filled philosopher Spinoza believed) immanent, the universe itself as Pantheistic God.

We are the spinoff and worshipful offspring of Almighty Creation, its majesty, immensity, beauty, inexhaustible potency and impenetrable mystery that generates in us redemptive, all-embracing love, *agape,* including our love

for one another. It is our gift of salvation, an ever-enriching blessing the more we share it..

About the Author

Saul Rosenthal is a retired teacher, having taught at Midwest universities in Michigan, Illinois, and Indiana. He is also a journalist, an author of several books, and a playwright. Two of his ten plays have won awards in national competitions.

Printed in the United States
By Bookmasters